LET GOD FORGIVE HIM

Let God

Forgive Him

By

Ebony Nicole

Ebony Nicole

Let God Forgive Him

Copyright © 2014 Ebony N. Freeman

All rights reserved. All names, characters, and incidents depicted in this book are products of the author's imagination or are used fictitiously. Any resemblance to actual events, locales, organizations, or persons, living or dead, is entirely coincidental, and beyond the intent of the author or the publisher.

No part of this book may be reproduced or transmitted in any form or by any means, electronic or mechanical, including photocopying, recording, or by any information storage and retrieval system, without permission in writing from the publisher.

Printed in the United States

ISBN-13: 978-0692312292 ISBN-10: 0692312293

Printed by Createspace 2014

Published by BlaqRayn Publishing Plus 2014

~Dedication~

I am dedicating my works to those of you who have been through any type of struggle(s) and didn't think there was a way out. Each day that you wake up, it only makes you stronger for what's to come. Never give up the fight because the struggle will never end.

Ebony Nicole

~Acknowledgments~

This writing journey has not been easy and I have so much to learn but, I would like to sincerely thank all the people that have stood by me. There are too many to name names; you know who you are; even those of you that have heard about my work and took a chance. I couldn't thank you enough for giving me and my work a chance. Through each story I create, I want to help someone in the process. This is what it is about for me as a writer. When you read one of my books and spread the word; that means the world to me and again I thank you.

Let God Forgive Him

Ebony Nicole

LET GOD FORGIVE HIM

Touched

I was touched at a young age.

I still don't know how I can live with this pain,

But I still love this man.

I suffered through the most precious years of my life.

Trying to find my way and do what was right,

But all I could see was the pain inside.

Holding in tears that damaged pride,

Crying day in and day out as the world passed me by.

No one knew of all this pain and hurt I had inside

As I did things out of anger or just because I thought I could.

I even did shit 'cause I thought it would make me feel good.

Ebony Nicole

I didn't have the guidance I needed to make it through another day,

Didn't even have the courage to pray and say what my heart really wanted to say.

So, here I am, still lost and trying to find my way,

But, through it all, I must stand.

Never again will I be touched by another man.

Chapter 1: Jewels' Confession

"Mama, please, don't make me go back there!" Jewels pleaded.

"Go where, baby?" Shelia asked her daughter.

"My daddy's house," Jewels answered as tears fell from her eyes.

She looked at her mother, but the words wouldn't come out. Shelia opened the car door for her daughter, but she didn't force her to talk under the condition she was in. All kinds of thoughts were going through Shelia's head as she drove down Martin Luther King Jr. Drive, towards their apartment. Shelia glanced at Jewels every now and then to make sure she was okay. It had been a while since Jewels had lived with her mother.

Shelia was in the process of getting her life back on track after having been strung out on drugs. Shelia had made the decision to let Jewels stay with her father until things got better for her. She was now in her second year of being clean and sober, so getting her babies back was the next thing on her list of things to do. Drugs had consumed her life at one point, but Shelia was now a perfect example of someone who had overcome her addiction. She was showing the world that only the strong survived.

Pulling up to their apartment, Jewels followed Shelia's lead but took slow strides with her head hanging down. Shelia grabbed Jewels' chin, forcing her to look up, and said, "Baby, hold your head up."

Now headed up the stairs, Shelia noticed that Jewels had stopped walking. She thought she'd heard her say something.

"Mama, he rapped me, and I don't want to live with him anymore. Please, can I come back to live with you now?" Jewels said.

LET GOD FORGIVE HIM

Shelia felt as if her legs were about to give out, so she held on to the rail of the stairs. She could see the pain in her daughter's eyes and knew she wasn't lying. Her hands shook as she attempted to make it up the stairs to unlock the door. Jewels was crying, trying to think of a way to tell her mother how her daddy had raped her. She was eight years old when it had happened, too young to understand anything.

Having to hold this secret for four years had damn near killed her, but this was the perfect time to tell her mama what had taken place. They both cried as Jewels poured her heart out to her mother. The next day, Shelia took Jewels to the doctor for a full check-up.

This was the beginning of a long journey.

Chapter 2: The Teen Clinic

Shelia and Jewels woke up early the next morning and went to the clinic. When they arrived, they found that the clinic was packed. Jewels felt so uncomfortable being there, but she knew this was something she had to do. Shelia signed her in, and they waited for the doctor to call for them. At the sight of the doctor, Jewels thought she would shit bricks because he was a man. After they entered the exam room, Dr. Michaels instructed Jewels to undress and put on the hospital gown. She was so nervous. Dr. Michaels could tell something was wrong when he returned to the room.

"What's the matter, Ms. Jewels?" he asked.

"Um, nothing really, but may I have a female doctor to perform my exam, please?" Jewels asked timidly.

LET GOD FORGIVE HIM

"Sure," Dr. Michaels replied. Then, he turned and walked out of the room.

Ten minutes later, Dr. Bryant walked in, followed by Shelia. There was no way she would let her baby go through this alone. Quietly sitting in the chair next to Jewels, Sheila waited as the exam took place. Dr. Bryant was very nice, and her smile lit up the whole room. Jewels felt comfortable in her care. She and Jewels talked during the whole procedure and time seemed to pass faster. By the time Jewels started to get impatient, her exam was over. Dr. Bryant told them to hold tight while the test results came back. Jewels didn't know how to feel as she waited. Shelia was on the edge, too. Many thoughts were running through her head at one time. When Dr. Bryant returned, Shelia stood up to hear the results, and Jewels closed her eyes.

"Well, Ms. Shelia, everything is okay. All of your daughter's test results came back negative. If you have any questions, you may ask me, and I'll assist you."

"Oh no, Dr. Bryant. You have been wonderful, and my baby and I are happy about the results."

"Thank you, Dr. Bryant. You are the best," Jewels replied.

Following her mother out of the clinic to the car, Jewels was happy that the exam was over and that she was okay.

Chapter 3: The Confrontation

Shelia was so hurt inside, knowing that her daughter had been raped by the man she had married when she was only twenty years old. Years had gone by. They hadn't been together in a long time. At night, she cried as she imagined the pain that Jewels must have felt. This was her daughter, her last child to be born. How could this shit have happened? A week after she took Jewels to the hospital, Shelia tried to talk to Jewels about the incident, but Jewels didn't want to relive the pain. She had shut down all together. Her reply was simply, "Ask my daddy. He will tell you."

Shelia understood that Jewels didn't want to talk, but she asked her how she would feel if her father, Walter, came over, so that Shelia and Walter could talk. Shelia promised that, if, at any time, Jewels didn't feel comfortable, she would make him leave. Jewels was okay with that. She just wanted to get it over with. Shelia called Walter on his cell phone several times but only got his voice-mail. Shelia left a message and waited for him to call back. Later that day, Walter called back, but Jewels wasn't home.

"We need to talk to you, and don't bring anybody with you," Shelia told Walter.

"Talk to me about what?" Walter questioned.

"Don't ask me shit! Just get over here!" Shelia said and hung up the phone.

Shelia paged Jewels to let her know she needed to come home. They entered their special code: 2111. Jewels walked into the apartment, and, shortly after, Walter showed up. She didn't open her mouth. She just sat down next to her mother on the sofa. Shelia grabbed her hand. Jewels laid her head on her mother's shoulder.

LET GOD FORGIVE HIM

"Walter, what have you done? Jewels said that you raped when she was eight years old, and I know my baby wouldn't lie on you. She loves you. You are her father."

Walter sat there with a surprised look on his face as Jewels started to cry.

"What are you talking about? You called me over here for this bullshit? She is lying. She's just saying this because she wants to come back and live with you," Walter answered, trying to explain.

"You a muthafuckin' lie, Walter. You know Jewels wouldn't lie on you like that. How could you do that to our baby? Why?" Shelia screamed.

By this time, she was up in his face. She wanted him to feel their pain.

"You are a sick son of a bitch! You need to get some fucking help! I can't believe you, Walter. Now, you aren't even man enough to tell me what you did. Get the fuck out of my house! We don't ever want to see you again, and, if you lay one finger on Jewels ever again, I will kill you my damn self."

Neither Jewels nor Walter had ever seen Shelia so mad. Her eyes were red as fire. Her face displayed a scowl that was unrecognizable. Walter walked out the door, feeling lower than the dirt on his dusty-ass tennis shoes. His secret was out!

Chapter 4: Jewels' Smelling Herself

The day after Walter left, Jewels' and Shelia's lives changed drastically. Jewels tried to find her way, while Shelia fell deeper into depression. Despite all the shit Jewels had started to get into, Shelia didn't go back to the streets. That was what had started this whole mess in the first place. While she was on drugs, it was best that her babies live with Walter. His life wasn't so out of order, or, at least, that was what she had thought. At that time, he'd had a place to live, and he was responsible enough to make sure they went to school the way they needed to.

No matter how hard she tried, Shelia couldn't reach her daughter the way she needed to. It seemed as if Jewels was getting worse. The things she did and said just weren't right. Shelia could remember one day in particular when Jewels did not come home right after school. By the time Shelia got home, Jewels should have been somewhere around their apartments. As the day went by, there was no sign of Jewels. Shelia called everybody she could think of. Nobody knew where Jewels was and they hadn't talked to her. Shelia was so worried. It was almost eleven P.M. when Jewels walked into the house. Shelia was livid! Jewels walked in without a care in the world, went straight to her room, and closed the door behind her. Shelia was right on her heels, but the door slammed in her face. After smelling the strong aroma of weed and alcohol, she realized that Jewels was high. Shelia turned the knob and opened the door.

"Where have you been all day, Jewels?"

Jewels wouldn't even look at her mother. She held her head down while she talked.

"I was at my friend's house," Jewels lied.

"What fucking friend? Because I called Rhonda and Mesha, and neither one of them talked to you today."

"I wasn't with them. I was with my other friends. You don't know them," Jewels said, rolling her eyes and smacking her lips.

Now, Shelia didn't play that shit. If you wanted to be grown or act like it, then you would be treated like it. Shelia was a short lady; she stood about 5'2", had dark skin and short hair. She was very beautiful, but she didn't take any shit from nobody. Before Jewels knew what had happened to her, she was holding the left side of her face where Shelia had slapped her.

"First of all, you are thirteen years old! You will not be coming in and out of my fucking house like you pay bills up in here! I want your ass in here when the street lights come on and no later. Do you hear me?"

"Yeah."

It was on again. Shelia grabbed her by

the collar of her shirt and pulled her off the bed.

"Girl, I'm not one of your friends! I'm your mother! The least you can do is show me some fucking respect. I don't know what your problem is, but you won't disrespect me."

Tears fell from Jewels' eyes. Shelia left the room, swinging the door wide open.

"And don't close any fucking doors around here! Oh! And another thing! I smell that weed and shit on your clothes. You better leave that shit alone if you know what I know."

Jewels' high was blown. She lay across her bed and thought about the day she had spent with her man. Shelia worked two jobs, so she was never home. She would get Jewels up in the morning and drop her off at school. Some days, Jewels would catch the school bus with Rhonda and Mesha. These were her friends that lived in the same apartment complex. They were tight, did everything together, whether they were cutting school, hanging out with boys or somewhere trying to smoke weed and drink.

Rhonda was the quiet one. She had brown skin and long hair down her back. She had a body that drove the niggas crazy. It was "just right" as they would say. Mesha was attractive, too. She was short with dark skin, brown eyes, and she was thick. They liked to show off their bodies, and guys always thought they were older. Jewels, on the other hand, didn't like to show off hers. She would hide her shape under baggy clothes most times. Jewels' self-esteem was low due to what her father had done. She tried to conceal this by looking for love in all the wrong places. Just like her man that Shelia didn't know about. Terry was twenty-two. He would pick Jewels up and go back to his house. That was where she spent most of her time. To Jewels, Terry was just what she needed. He gave her everything she wanted, and he felt good, getting pussy whenever he wanted it. Jewels had told him she was seventeen, and he believed her. Besides, under the baggy clothes, she had a body that would fool anybody. Jewels was built like her mother. Shelia had thick thighs, a round ass, and she had gotten her big breasts from her grandmother. She had chocolate skin, and she usually wore her hair short. She was sexy to say the least.

On the day she met Terry, she, Rhonda, and Mesha were standing at the bus stop, headed downtown. Terry rolled up in his Caprice with tented windows, rims, the whole nine. Rhonda and Mesha weren't paying any attention when he called Jewels to his car. They exchanged numbers and had been kicking it ever since. You couldn't tell Jewels shit. Terry had her wide open, and she was indeed, smelling herself.

Chapter 5: Walter's Other Family

After Walter left Shelia's house, he returned to the apartment that he shared with his girlfriend Robin and her daughter Shawn. Jewels had met Robin, and she didn't like the bitch. There was something about her. Shawn was cool, though, and they hung out from time to time. Walter had had a lot of women. That was one reason Shelia had left him years ago. He and Robin had been together for a while, but Walter still came around Shelia and her family. Robin didn't care for Shelia, and Shelia couldn't stand her ass, either. It wasn't the same when Walter came around. Everybody seemed to stray away because he was still using drugs and drinking. When he was high, Walter wouldn't come around his family. Most times, Robin wouldn't see him, either, for days at a time. All of Walter's family lived in Decatur, so that was his hang out spot.

Sometimes, he would try contacting his kids, but to no avail.

Jewels was the baby. There were three others besides her. Basically, all of their hearts had turned cold towards Walter because of what he had done to Jewels. Nobody trusted him. The two oldest children, Monica and Chris, had kids of their own, and they weren't comfortable with them being around Walter. Richard was also doing his own thing, so he stayed away, too. Walter always found himself trying to be a part of their lives, even the grand-kids, but they barely knew him.

Chapter 6: Shelia Finds Out

Shelia remained focused, even after that first incident with Jewels. She noticed that Jewels' attitude had changed and that she was getting thick. At that point, she didn't have time to pay it too much attention because Shelia had to continue to work and maintain their household. Things were hectic for her. Although her boyfriend helped sometimes, Shelia picked up a second job to make ends meet. She didn't want to depend on any man to take care of her.

Miles called her one day after she got off work to see if she wanted to go out to dinner. She agreed, so he picked her up around 6:30 P.M., but, just before they got ready to go, Shelia realized she hadn't seen Jewels all day. She had bought her a cell phone, which she used to call Jewels several times, but Jewels never answered.

Shelia wanted to just enjoy her evening, so Shelia left with Miles. It was nice, but Miles wasn't a very romantic man, so they weren't out long. When they returned to Shelia's apartment, Shelia spotted Jewels coming out of the house with a man behind her.

At the sight of her mother, Jewels' eyes grew to the size of saucers. She pushed Terry back into the house, trying her best to hide him, but it was too late. Shelia flew up the stairs, headed straight for the both of them.

"Who the fuck is this grown-ass man you got up in my house?"

"He's my friend, Mama!"

Shelia turned to Terry with angry eyes.

"So, you're fucking my daughter? I'm going to have your ass arrested for statutory rape. She is too young for you!"

"I really like your daughter, ma'am, and

she is old enough. I'm only twenty-two years old."

"Twenty-two"! Jewels is fourteen. Her birthday just passed in March!"

Jewels and Terry stood there, dumbfounded. Then, Terry walked out the door. Jewels looked at her mother, who had tears in her eyes. She knew she was hurting Shelia, breaking her heart. Shelia walked to Jewels' room. The smell of sex was all in the air. The covers on the bed were thrown everywhere. The fan was blowing, making the scent even stronger. Shelia looked at Jewels. Pain was evident on her face. That night, Shelia knew she had to take action by putting Jewels on some kind of birth control. She was not ready for her baby to have a baby.

After that night, Jewels' behavior only got worse. It got to the point that Shelia wanted to send her somewhere to get some help. Jewels was off the chain. Nothing stopped her from getting what she wanted— be it sex, drugs, or alcohol. All of it was at her fingertips. She made sure there was always a nigga around to give it to her; Terry was no longer the only one she was fucking. They messed around for a while, but, eventually, Jewels wanted more, and she was going to get it. There were lessons in the streets that Jewels learned; some, harder than others. Jewels had some run-ins with a couple of dudes that had missions of their own, and her mission was to not become a victim. That was a position she didn't want to be in ever again. Jewels wanted to always be in control of what happened or didn't happen to her, but she didn't always come out on top.

She had met one dude from the Islands. They had gone out a few times, and he always gave her money. He wasn't attractive at all, but he had money. Isaac was his name. He thought Jewels was sexy, and he knew she was

LET GOD FORGIVE HIM

young. He lived in the same apartment complex, so it was easy for Jewels to get away. She and her girls would chill at his spot, while he was at work during the day. After a while Isaac became possessive, only wanting Jewels to come over by herself, but Jewels wasn't comfortable with that. Besides, she really didn't know Isaac. That was why her girls rolled with her.

One night, Jewels decided to go over to his place, alone, thinking she could trust him. She showed up around 7:30 P.M., looking good enough to eat with fresh braids and her nails and toes done. She thought she and Isaac were going to chill, but Isaac had other plans for the night. As they sat there drinking one of Jewels' favorite drinks, Hen & Coke, and watching T.V, Isaac began to feel up Jewels. It felt good, but that was not what she had come over for, so Jewels kept pushing Isaac away. He didn't like the rejection, so he let her know.

"Bitch, you think I've been doing all of this for you for nothing?" Isaac said in his thick accent.

Jewels was shocked. She could tell that this situation was about to get ugly, real fast. Always fly at the mouth, Jewels got jazzy with him, saying, "Nigga, what the fuck do you mean? I'm telling you that I don't want to fuck you. You did that shit 'cause you wanted to. I don't owe you anything."

"See! That's where you are wrong. You are going to give me some of this young pussy, and you are going to give it to me tonight!"

Jewels knew he was serious from the look in his eyes, but she was willing to fight if she had to. That was exactly what she did because Isaac was determined to get some pussy, and Jewels wasn't having it.

Isaac threw himself on top of Jewels. Then, he grabbed a handful of her braids as he attempted to take her shirt off, then her pants.

LET GOD FORGIVE HIM

The braids felt like they were coming from the root of her head since she had just got them done. He pulled harder. Jewels kicked her legs and clawed at his face as she tried to get loose. This only enraged Isaac. He became more aggressive, pulling her hair harder and putting his elbow against her neck. His big hand was now in her pants, rubbing roughly on her clit as he sucked her nipples, attempting to get her in the mood. Isaac went down to eat Jewels' pussy. By this time, she had come up with a plan.

Suddenly, she was in the mood, but Isaac had a price to pay. Thinking that Jewels was okay with it, Isaac continued to eat her pussy. She was pretending to be all into it, too, moaning and calling his name. Just before she was about to cum, Jewels grabbed a vase from the end table and hit Isaac over the head with it. He didn't know what had hit him as he grabbed his head in an attempt to stop the blood that was now gushing out all over the place.

Jewels jumped up quickly, pulling her pants up. Isaac was still down on the floor. When he looked up, Jewels kicked the shit out of him in the face, causing even more blood to appear. Isaac was trying to get his bearings. He weakly charged Jewels, barely knocking her down. She was ready, though. Strength comes from nowhere when you're mad. Jewels used that strength to her advantage. Everything in sight went flying at Isaac's head or wherever she could get a hit in. Isaac was down to the point where Jewels could get away. She ran to the front door and down the stairs to Mesha's house.

Mesha saw how distraught her friend was and called Rhonda. They didn't ask any questions. Isaac was going to pay for whatever he had done to their friend. All three of them went back to Isaac's house, but he wouldn't open the damn door, threatening to call the police if they didn't leave. They didn't fuck around with the police, so they left but not but not before messing up Isaac's car, which was parked out front. He had a black on black Camry, nothing spectacular, but it was his car. Mesha went to get two cartons of eggs while Rhonda and Jewels got some bricks and blades.

By the time they were done, the paint, windows, and tires on Isaac's car were fucked up. Isaac would definitely not be driving his car to work the next morning. The neighbors watched the girls in action, but it was too dark to make out any faces. Oh, well! Jewels had told him he would pay. The whole time, Jewels thought about that day when she eight years old, wishing she had had the courage to fight back then, the way she did with Isaac.

Chapter 7: Jewels' Way or No Way

The incident with Isaac taught Jewels several lessons. The number one lesson was to do shit on her terms. From then on, everybody she fucked had to be doing something for her. Shit! Everybody wanted something, and Jewels wanted money. Her girls didn't agree with her, often times, comparing her to a trick. Jewels didn't care. Every nigga in her circle had a purpose. It worked for a long time. She had money, flashy clothes, and jewelry to show off. Her plan was to never give anyone her heart. Even the dudes that were really feeling her didn't have a chance.

Terry was still around, but they didn't see much of each other anymore. Jewels was doing her thing and loving it. Every day, she learned something new, but, through it all, she got what she wanted. There was one dude Jewels loved to fuck with— Mark, tall with dark skin and brown eyes. He always came around smelling and looking good. Eating pussy was his profession. Mark drove a black Chevy with the blue strips down the middle. Jewels loved riding in his car. He played the music loud and it made her ass vibrate against the seats. She could hear him long before he pulled into her apartment when he came to pick her up.

She, Rhonda, and Mesha were sitting outside on this day, right after school. Mark pulled up and told them to get in. They rode to his apartment, which was not too far from theirs. Rhonda and Mesha already knew what it was. They knew that they wouldn't be going home anytime soon.

At Mark's spot, they did whatever they wanted. Jewels went straight to his bedroom. She flopped down on his king size bed. The sheets were fresh from the dryer, smelled of Bounty fresh. Jewels loved his apartment because everything was in place. She grabbed the remote and turned on the TV to see what was on. Mark came in twenty minutes later and smacked Jewels on the ass.

"What's up, baby?"

"Nothing.   What's up with you?"

"Shit! You know me. Got to make this money, baby."

Jewels loved the sound of that because Mark made sure she was straight, even when he was out making that money.

"That's what's up.   As long as you don't forget about me, we good."

"You already know."

Marked laid next to Jewels and grabbed a blunt from his night stand.   He rolled one up as they watched a movie.   Jewels loved Lifetime, so that was the first channel she went to. One of the reasons she liked Mark was that he didn't always want to fuck her.   They would sometimes, but he was older, so it wasn't always on his mind. Mark and Jewels laid there and smoked their blunt. Then, Jewels got up to use the restroom. On the way, she checked on her girls.

"Are y'all good?"

"Hell, yeah, bitch! You know we good!" Rhonda said.

"Yeah, I'm good," Mesha said. She was sitting on the sofa, looking sleepy. The two of them had helped themselves to Mark's bar that he had set up in his dining room area. He had all kinds of shit in there, from Hennessy to Bacardi. Mesha's favorite drink was a Long Island Iced Tea. She had made a big glass of it. Rhonda had made a small glass of Hen & Coke. When she saw that they were good, Jewels went to the restroom, then returned to the bedroom. Marked was still laying in the same place she had left him. The weed had taken effect on Jewels. She laid down on top of him, kissing him on the neck as she put her hand down his pants. Jewels liked to see the look on Mark's face as she played with his dick. Stroking it up and down, he began to moan, returning the favor. Mark could feel Jewels wetness as he inserted one finger, then two, into her tunnel with slow movements. It felt so good. Jewels wanted him to eat her pussy because he did it so well.

"Baby, I want to feel your tongue on my pussy."

"You know that you don't have to tell me that. I know what you want, baby," he said, lifting her up above his head. Mark sat Jewels right down on his face. She gyrated her hips against Mark's tongue. The feeling was intensified by the weed they had smoked.

Rhonda got up and turned on the radio to drown out the moans coming from the bedroom. She didn't want to hear them having sex that night.

LET GOD FORGIVE HIM

When Mark and Jewels were done, Rhonda and Mesha were knocked out. They all stayed at Mark's apartment for the night. They knew they would have some explaining to do when they got home.

Ebony Nicole

Part 2

LET GOD FORGIVE HIM

"Get Away"

I want to get away

And hide from the pain

And the shame that I feel. This is a daily battle that I fight,

And it just doesn't feel right,

Having to be reminded and to see this man every day.

Somebody tell me which way is the getaway.

Take me there and leave me for this pain.

I'm hurting to no end.

I don't want to be mean,

But what did I do to deserve this?

When do I get a break?

Because this is something I can no longer take.

I want to get away.

Chapter 8: I'm eighteen. I'm Grown.

Shelia and Jewels moved to Edgewood when Jewels turned eighteen. Shelia felt like Jewels needed new surroundings, and she needed an apartment based on her income. Jewels wasn't happy. This move put them closer to Walter. Once they had settled in, he came around all the time now that they were in Decatur.

Jewels was a senior at Crim High School, but she was so unfocused. There was too much going on, so she ended up going to night classes. Being introduced to new people brought new issues. Half of the time, Jewels didn't attend classes at all. She, also, worked as a cashier at McDonald's. This was where she met Stacey. Jewels had never liked girls before, but there was something about Stacey's personality. Stacey would come up there to get something to eat, and Jewels would always look for her, too. They flirted whenever Stacey came through. Then, Jewels saw her at school. This came as a surprise to Jewels because she thought Stacey was older. They would go to their classes together. Jewels really liked this girl, but how the hell would she explain this to her family and friends.

Rhonda was the first person Jewels told. She was cool, although she asked a lot of questions. She just wanted to make sure this was just a phase that Jewels was going through, but she didn't care either way. The more Stacey and Jewels were around each other, the more their attraction grew. This explained Jewels' absences at school. She and Stacey would go to Stacey's house even on the nights that Jewels was supposed to be at school. They had a lot in common. Their birthdays were even in the same month.

Shelia dropped Jewels off at school one night with plans to pick her up when her class was over. As soon as Shelia pulled off, Jewels called Stacey to meet her half way. They went to Stacey's house that night, and Jewels had her first lesbian experience. Scared was an understatement to describe how Jewels felt. Stacey took her time, but Jewels still felt like shitting bricks. Stacey put her lips to Jewels'. Stacey thought they felt soft, and Jewels made sure they were. Although she never wore a lot of make-up, she always had her lip gloss, though. Jewels pulled away, afraid of this feeling, yet Stacey was persistent and pushed forward.

"You don't have to be scared. I'm not going to hurt you," Stacey told her while looking into Jewels' eyes.

"I know. I've never done anything like this before."

"It's cool. I will show you."

They were in Stacey's living room. Her mother wasn't home. Jewels' mind was in a thousand places, but the things Stacey did brought her back to the present. Stacey's hands on Jewels' skin made her body quiver as Stacey made circles on the small of her back. With the other hand, she ran her fingers through Jewels' short hair. Jewels relaxed and got comfortable. She laid on her stomach as Stacey lay on top of her. With closed eyes, Jewels imagined how Stacey would make her feel if she licked her clit. Thoughts became reality as Stacey got up and turned Jewels over to face her. She kissed her from head to toe, making sure to linger in the spots that would make Jewels hot. Her breasts were the perfect place to start. Jewels had big breast. They were nice, round, and succulent, just the way Stacey liked them. Jewels gasped with every touch. Being pleased by another female felt crazy. What would this mean when they were done? Would Jewels be a lesbian? How would she tell her mother? Stacey's tongue on her clit made Jewels forget about all of that. She enjoyed the time while it lasted. That tongue was lethal, making circles around Jewels' clit, going in and out of her hot tunnel. Sucking, nibbling, as her fingers found their way inside Jewels' wet deep. Stacey pulled her fingers out, then put them to Jewels' lips. She was so hot that she stuck her tongue out to taste her own juices. When Stacey was done, Jewels lay on the sofa unable to move. She just laid there in her own wetness. Something was wrong, though. It was too wet under her. Stacey cuddled up next to Jewels.

"Are you okay?"

"Yes, but why is it so wet under me, and why is my body shacking?"

"You are good. That's called an orgasm."

"What? I have never heard of that before."

Stacey smiled at Jewels, thinking her reaction was cute.

LET GOD FORGIVE HIM

"There's nothing to be worried about. If a person can't give you one, then they are not doing shit."

These were the last words Jewels heard before drifting off to sleep. In a peaceful slumber, she was disturbed by the ringing of her cell phone. Shit! It was her mother calling. Jewels was late getting back to the school. It was 10:30 P.M. Her class had ended at 8:30 P.M. Jewels jumped up and put her clothes on. Stacey heard her moving around and came to see what the problem was. After explaining, she and Stacey rushed out the door. It was a sight to see because both of them were short, but their little legs were moving as they raced up Memorial Drive. Stacey stood near the stairs while Jewels went toward the school. They gave each other a quick peck on the lips and parted ways. It was pitch black. There were no students, lights, or cars, except for Shelia's.

"Damn!" Jewels said to herself while

walking to the car.

As soon as she got in, Jewels started explaining. She knew Shelia was angry.

"I'm sorry, Mama. I went to my friend's house because we got out of class early tonight."

Shelia knew Jewels was lying. She had been sitting there way before her class was supposed to end.

"Girl, I don't want to hear that shit. You know what time I pick you up. Your ass should have been waiting for me, not the other way around. Knowing you, you probably didn't even go to class tonight."

Jewels knew her mother was right. The rest of the ride home was silent. As soon as they got there, Jewels went to her room and called Stacey. They talked on the phone for the rest of the night until falling asleep with the phone to their ears.

LET GOD FORGIVE HIM

Months went by, Stacey and Jewels decided to become a couple. It was a funny feeling at first since Jewels didn't want anybody to know, especially her family. They only hung out at school or at Stacey's house. A lot of their friends knew since they were always together.

After a year of dating, Jewels broke up with Stacey, upset about what she was hearing around the school. The rumor was that Jewels was spending all of her money buying shit for Stacey. Stacey was always a dresser, decked out in a fresh Dickey outfit with the Ones to match. It didn't help that Stacey got a lot of attention from other girls.

Jewels really didn't like that, but Stacey was popular. Everybody liked to be around her, but Jewels didn't see it that way, so, to Jewels, it was best if she just ended the whole relationship. Stacey was mad, but what could she do? She knew how Jewels felt. They talked about it all the time. Now, all they had was a friendship.

Chapter 9: What a Mistake?

Jewels cut off her relationship with Stacey and met her biggest mistake, Tiffany. Whenever she came around, Shelia would look at her funny, wondering why she was hanging around all of a sudden. Shelia couldn't stand Tiffany. She hung around the dope boys on their street and didn't go to school. She even looked like a boy — brown skin that was cut with muscles and definition, dreads that framed an angular, hard face, and baggy clothes that hung from her boyishly shaped body. You could hardly tell her apart from the boys.

One day, Tiffany and Jewels were sitting on Jewels' front porch when Shelia pulled up. Jewels was sitting on Tiffany's lap, laughing and talking shit, oblivious to Shelia's presence. Shelia was confused but didn't embarrass Jewels. She simply told her that she needed to talk to her inside. Jewels got up and walked in behind her mother, waving goodbye to Tiffany.

"Jewels, what the hell was that about?"

"Oh, nothing, Ma. That's just my friend, but I'm not gay."

"I didn't say you were, but something is going on. You were sitting on that girl's lap."

"I mean I like her, but only as a friend."

"I hope that's all it is because I wouldn't know how to feel if you told me you did like girls."

Little did Shelia know that Jewels had already crossed that line with Stacey. When Shelia was done talking, Jewels went back outside to find Tiffany. Tiffany's mother, Claudia, was the first person to know about the two of them messing around. Jewels wasn't ready to tell Shelia yet. She knew it would break her heart, but she knew she had to tell her. Since she was always the one to write, Jewels decided to write her mother a note.

Dear Mama,

I'm sorry for lying to you about Tiffany and me. We are a couple. I hope this doesn't change your love for me, but I really do like her. Even if I decide to date females from this point on, I hope I will always be your baby girl.

Love Always,

Jewels

Shelia was dropping Jewels off at Rhonda's house when she received this note. Jewels handed it to her and quickly got out of the car. After opening it up and reading it, tears filled Shelia's eyes. She rolled down the window and told Jewels to come back. She hadn't even made it to Rhonda's walkway yet. The tears in Shelia's eyes indicated that she had read the note. Jewels didn't make it to

Rhonda's house. As soon as she got in the car, Shelia pulled off, headed straight for Tiffany's. She wasn't hard to find. Shelia found her walking out of the driveway.

"I want you to stay the fuck away from my daughter! You are nothing but trouble! I don't want to catch you around my house, either!"

She saw Tiffany trying to say something, but Shelia had already pulled off. What she needed to say had been said, and that was that. Talking to Jewels felt like a waste of time. It seemed that her mind was made up. Jewels soon learned that she should have listen to Shelia.

The beginning of Jewels and Tiffany's relationship was cool, but sugar turned to shit fast as Tiffany became verbally and physically abusive. Nothing Jewels did was good enough for her. Either way, Jewels would get it. The first time Tiffany hit Jewels it wasn't a big deal. She didn't pay it much attention. Tiffany had apologized and promised not to do it again. Believing that lie and all the rest that followed it only made things worse. Jewels covered up the bruises from the abuse to protect Tiffany. She didn't want anybody to know that side of her. Jewels really thought that things would change for the better. She would stay at Tiffany's house to hide the bruises from her mother.

One time, Tiffany had sucked one of Jewels' cheeks to the point that it turned a purple. She said that nobody was going to want Jewels when they saw it, but Jewels was confused because— Hell!— it seemed that Tiffany didn't want her either. So, what was the point? Then, everything was supposedly worked out whenever Tiffany had sex with Jewels. That was her way of saying "I'm sorry".

Fighting became their daily routine. Most

times, Jewels wouldn't fight Tiffany back. She knew what love was but had it mixed up with lust because this couldn't be what love was about. When Jewels did fight back, that only made Tiffany angrier, subjecting Jewels to more abuse. Her life was a living hell. Jewels wished she had never met Tiffany and missed what she'd had with Stacey. One thing was for certain, Stacey had never laid a finger on Jewels. Sometimes, Jewels would call Stacey, but, if Tiffany found out she was talking to anybody, that would have been a fight. Tiffany would check her cell phone just to see who Jewels was talking to. Any little thing started a fight.

Claudia was even watching Jewels like a hawk. To them, she couldn't be trusted, but Tiffany could do no wrong. Claudia would vouch for Tiffany even when she knew the shit Tiffany did was dead-ass wrong, but that was her baby. It wasn't long before Tiffany started

LET GOD FORGIVE HIM

fucking with other bitches, leading Jewels by a string.

Many times, Jewels wanted to get out of the situation but couldn't find it in her heart to walk away. Tiffany didn't give a fuck. She talked to bitches on the phone. Then, she got bold, and they started coming to pick her up right on their street, knowing Jewels would be there whenever she got back. It was never the same bitch. Tiffany had started smoking weed which was not good for Jewels. The abuse became more frequently. Feeling helpless, Jewels wore the scars daily. She wanted to tell Shelia what was going on, but how? That would only make the situation worse for her.

Tiffany and Jewels were sitting outside when a car pulled up. Tiffany got up and walked to the car. She kissed the girl in the driver's seat. A dude was on the passenger side. Jewels was mad as fuck and tired of the disrespect. She got up and walked to Tiffany.

"What the fuck are you doing?"

"Man, go on! I don't have time for your shit!"

"You act like I'm not sitting right here. Who is this bitch?"

"Bitch, fuck you"! You ain't shit to me! Get the fuck out of my face before I hurt your ass out here!"

Jewels was hurt, but she wasn't about to stand there like a fool.

"No bitch! Fuck you. I'm tired of your shit. This has been going on for too long."

Jewels slapped Tiffany on the back of her head. The girl in the car laughed as Tiffany turned around and smashed Jewels in the face. Jewels swung non-stop and hit Tiffany in her face.

Grabbing a hold of Jewels, Tiffany threw Jewels to the ground. As she fell, she broke one of the heels she had on. They matched

LET GOD FORGIVE HIM

Jewels' cute, blue and white Capri outfit.

Tiffany didn't give a fuck how cute Jewels was. Her mission was to fuck Jewels up. She grabbed Jewels by her hair and hit her in the face so hard that it drew blood. Jewels felt the blood running down her face.

Tiffany was in a zone. Every hit connected, and they were hard, but Jewels was not taking it lying down. For every hit she received, she gave one back. She wasn't a damn punching bag. As they fought in the middle of the street, the bitch in the car pulled off. Jewels was used to the fighting, but— Damn!— how was Tiffany going to play her like that? Finally, people came to break up the fight. Jewels was now down on the ground, and Tiffany was on top of her. Just before she balled up her fist to hit Jewels, Shelia came rushing through the crowd. Shelia grabbed Tiffany and pulled her off of her baby. She didn't know everything, but, from the looks of it, she could tell this had been going on for a while. Tiffany was disrespectful. She didn't even respect her own mother. She called Shelia every name in the book except a child of God, but Shelia was not the one for the bull. Tiffany was a child to her, so she wanted to talk to Claudia. She and Jewels walked across the street to their house and beat on the door.

"Who is it?" Claudia yelled.

"It's Shelia from across the street!"

As Claudia swung the door open, Shelia said, "I want you to keep your daughter away from mine. I didn't want them together in the first place."

"I can't do shit. You just tell Jewels to stop bringing her hot ass over my house every damn day, and you won't have to worry about it!"

"It doesn't matter whose house they are at. Tiffany doesn't need to be putting her hands on my baby. I'm not going to say it again. Next time, there won't be any talking!"

"Mama, let's just go. I'm done with Tiffany. You don't have to worry about it anymore," Jewels said.

Claudia was so childish. No matter what was said about Tiffany, she would take up for her. So, Claudia retorted, "You done with her? Tiffany don't want you anyway. You should have said she is done with your ass!"

As Jewels and Shelia walked away, Claudia slammed her front door. As they walked out towards the street, Jewels saw Tiffany getting into the same car that had pulled up before the fight. Jewels had been played for a fool, thinking Tiffany loved her, but that couldn't have been love. Her mind was made up. After that day, there would be no more of that bullshit.

Chapter 10: I'm Better Than That

It was time for Jewels to move on to better things. Out of the blue, she texted Stacey and invited her over. They were still friends but didn't talk as much as they used to. Jewels had changed her number, so Stacey didn't know who it was from the first text.

Jewels' text message read: **COME AND SEE ME.**

Stacey replied: **WHO IS THIS?**

Jewels wrote: **NIKKI, RED, PAM, AMBER, ALEXUS.**

Stacey replied: **WHAT THE HELL? WHO IS THIS? WHY ARE YOU PLAYING ON MY PHONE?**

When she didn't get a reply after the last text, Stacey decided to call the phone. She was surprised that it was Jewels. They talked for a while, catching up on the time that had

LET GOD FORGIVE HIM

been lost. Stacey had heard about all the shit Jewels was going through with Tiffany, but, at the time, she couldn't even reach out to her. There was no hesitation for Stacey to come over. It took Stacey damn near all day to get to Decatur since she lived in Marietta. Jewels met her at the Edgewood Candler Park Transit Station.

Stacey finally had a chance to meet Shelia. You would have thought they had known each other for years. Shelia instantly fell in love with Stacey's two handsome boys, Tay and Jay. They were so cute and playful.

Stacey spent the night. It was too much for them to travel back to Marietta. Plus, it was already late. Needless to say, they started dating again. Stacey always came to see Jewels. For some reason, Tiffany had a problem with this, but it was cool when she did it. Stacey and Jewels got their first apartment right before they turned nineteen. Now, Jewels knew what real love was. Shit wasn't easy for them, but they made it work. Jewels had a job with Stacey's cousin at Mrs. Winner's, while Stacey was getting welfare. It was only $280, but they worked it until things got better. Making a few adjustments, they soon became comfortable. Jewels knew Stacey loved her. They stayed down from that point on.

Chapter 11: The Pain Never Goes Away

Jewels did everything in her power to forget what had happened to her as a child, but, the older she got, the more pain she felt. These feelings resurfaced when Walter came around. Every time she and Stacey went to visit Shelia, he was there, and Jewels hated to see him.

Shelia explained to Jewels that her father was sick and that needed her help at this difficult time in his life. The drugs and alcohol had taken a toll on his health, and, if he didn't get help soon, it would kill him. On top of that, he had diabetes. Robin didn't give a damn enough to make sure he went to the doctor the way he needed to, so Walter had turned to Shelia for help. The more he came around, the better his condition became. He was now taking his medicine and going to the doctor, and Shelia had arranged for him to go to rehab.

It was time out for that shit, but, to Jewels, there was more going on than that. Walter's clothes were now at Shelia's house. Okay! Had he left his place and moved in? Jewels wondered.

Shelia asked Jewels how she would feel if she and Walter got back together. Jewels said she was okay with it. Who didn't want their parents together? But so much shit had happened between them that Jewels never thought it would ever happen. Jewels still loved her father, just didn't want to be around him. This was the topic for about a month straight. Jewels kept telling her mother that she was okay with it. Jewels figured Shelia had forgiven him for what he had done, the same way she thought she had. Shelia's happiness was more important. Besides, Jewels was grown and had moved out. She didn't have to deal with Walter. At least, that was what she thought, but Walter was everywhere she turned.

In Jewels' opinion, he was back to his old self. He was very headstrong. He felt that whatever he said was supposed to be done. He was always right, so this wasn't working for Jewels. She didn't respect her father, let alone listen to what he had to say. Walter had never said anything about Jewels' lifestyle, not to her face anyway, but he would make snide comments every now and then, like when was Jewels going to give him some grand-kids. Jewels hated when he said things like that. It always made her uncomfortable. Everybody knew Jewels wasn't trying to have any kids. She had things that she wanted to do. She wanted go to college and make a life for herself. Either way, Jewels wasn't trying to hear that shit. What could he possibly tell her after all this time? Fuck him and his feelings was Jewels' attitude because of all the pain she had to deal with because of him. She was still angry.

Ebony Nicole

As long as the pain was still inside, Jewels couldn't bring herself to forgive what her father had done. Everything Walter did or said was wrong in Jewels' eyes. To her, Walter had crossed the line, did things a father should never do. There wasn't a day that went by that Jewels didn't think about it, she remembered it like it was yesterday.

*****

I got up early to get ready for school. I attended Cleveland Avenue Elementary at the time. My daddy walked in the house, coming from a place unknown. As I walked around my room getting dressed, he walked up the stairs. I was excited to see him. Like always, I ran up to him.

"Hey Daddy! I'm getting ready for school all by myself."

LET GOD FORGIVE HIM

"That's daddy's big girl."

I noticed a look in my daddy's eyes, one that I had never saw before. Something was wrong, but I didn't care what it was that was my daddy. He went into his bedroom, which was right across from mine and closed the door.

I was ready now for school. My daddy called my name, and I quickly made my way to his room. He was lying on his bed.

"Yes Daddy?"

"Come here, Jewels. Daddy wants to see something."

"Okay, Daddy."

I walked over to my daddy's bed and sat next to him, waiting to see what he wanted. He got up and kissed me, but it wasn't a normal kiss, not the kind of a kiss a father is supposed to give his daughter. It didn't feel right. I didn't feel right. Something was definitely wrong.

"Daddy, what are you doing?"

Daddy didn't stop. Now, he was unbuttoning the buttons on my pink and white shirt.

"I just want to see if you have been messing with those little boys up there at your school."

"I haven't, Daddy. I don't even like them. They are always messing with me."

Daddy told me to lie down on the bed as he took my shirt and pants off. Everything was wrong, but what could I do? This was my daddy. I couldn't tell him no, and I was too young to understand what he was doing to me. He just promised that he wouldn't hurt me. When I saw Daddy taking off his clothes, I became terrified and started to cry.

"Daddy, what are you doing?" I asked, repeatedly.

There was something indescribable in his

eyes when he looked at my undeveloped body. There was nothing to see in my opinion. Daddy saw something, though. He put his fat hand down my little panties. I jumped out of fear. I was ready to run out of there and go to school, but it was too late for that. Daddy told me to touch his dick while he played in my virgin pussy. I felt like throwing up. This was not right, but I did what I was told not wanting to disappoint my daddy. Next, Daddy ate my pussy as if I was his woman. When he was done, Daddy climbed on top of me. I felt like bricks were weighing my body down as he forced his big dick inside of me. This was the most pain I had felt in my eight years of my life. There was no love in this. I cried, excruciating pain shot through my body. My daddy saw the tears in my eyes, knew he was hurting me, but he didn't stop. He promised that he wouldn't hurt me, and I believed him. Daddy kept pushing, trying to get deeper inside.

After a while, I couldn't feel anything. My whole body went numb. His dick didn't fit, but Daddy made it fit to his perfection as he moved his body on top of me. I closed my eyes, hoping that it would end, but it felt like forever that Daddy was on top of me, having his way, raping me.

When it was over, he rested his body on mine, exhausted from taking something that didn't belong to him. After a few minutes had passed, he got up and so did I, but my legs felt like Jell-O. The pain was unbearable. There was blood on the white sheets that covered Daddy's bed that matched the blood running down my legs. How could Daddy do this to me? He had promised that he wouldn't hurt me. I loved my daddy. He was the one who was supposed to protect me from others that tried to bring me harm.

I left my daddy's room and went to the

bathroom in an attempt to clean up the mess Daddy had made. I scrubbed my body hard, until I felt more pain. I wanted this to all just go away, but it wasn't that simple. It would take more than soap and water to clean up the damage that Daddy had done. I didn't realize how much until now.

*****

As everybody's life moved forward, Jewels was stuck not able to get away from the past. She wanted her parents back together, but being around Walter was too much of a reminder. Jewels felt like she was losing her mind. That was all she could think about, but being away from Walter made it a little easier. The sad thing was that this would always be a part of Jewels, no matter what she did. The sight of Walter or even hearing his name made her think of that day. Embedded in her heart's eyes, they resurfaced at times Jewels wished they wouldn't. Walter wasn't a man in her eyes. He was a coward. His opinion didn't matter to her. Jewels wasn't naive and young anymore. She could make her own decisions. Love was often falsely portrayed, but Jewels wouldn't be fooled again. Telling Shelia that she was okay with them getting back together was another big mistake Jewels had made.

Chapter 12: Always Feeling Like A Victim

Jewel never was able to come to terms with her childhood pain. Sometimes, she wondered if anybody really understood her and the way she felt. They couldn't possibly know if it never happened to them. Being grown and on her own didn't seem to help; shit was worse now. Jewels couldn't remember a time that she cried about this when she was a teenager. Why was it constantly affecting her now?

It made things hard for her relationship with Stacey, but their love was stronger than ever. When feelings of defeat, shame, and loneliness took hold of Jewels, Stacey was right there to comfort her. When Shelia was alone, Jewels talked to her, too. She did whatever it took to ease the pain. These were two people she could always depend on for love and support. Trust was out the door. Everybody was out to get Jewels if you let her tell it. Those that had hurt her in the past made it a hard path to reach her. She had a lock around her heart for protection, and it was hard to break. This shit had done a number on Jewels. It had consumed her life for so many years. Night time was the worst time. When the lights went off, the tears would come. There was something about darkness that triggered those feelings. Crying herself to sleep was the only thing that made her feel better. Jewels had always been taught not to hate anybody, but she damn sure hated what her father had done to her.

LET GOD FORGIVE HIM

A Letter to My Father

Dear Daddy,

You and I never talked about the day you raped me. Our lives have gone on as if nothing has happened. My heart is fighting all kinds of battles to this day, all because of you. You really messed me up in more ways than you will ever know. Yes, you may have apologized but that doesn't change the facts. That doesn't make me feel better inside. I shed tears damn near every day for something you call a mistake.

This whole experience has showed me what type of person I don't want to be and the type of people that I don't want around me.

Everybody blamed it on the fact that you were sick on drugs, but I don't want to put the blame there. I want you to take responsibility for this because you did it. I don't know the reason why and probably never will. When you came back into our lives, I had mixed emotions because I wasn't ready to face this. I was doing just fine without any reminders. I thought I had forgiven you until you came back.

I don't know why I thought you and Mama getting back together was a good idea. You and I are better off when we are not around each other. I don't trust you. Although you may be a changed man, you took away more than my virginity, and those things I can't get back. Our love to me is a lie.

If you ever read this book, I don't want you to think I wrote it to be spiteful. I just need a way out, a way out from the pain that you caused.

If you knew of all the tears I've shed, you would understand. I know when you see me, you see a smile on my face, but that's only a facade to shield my heart. It has been a long

LET GOD FORGIVE HIM

journey. My heart hasn't led me down the path to forgive you, so I will let God forgive you.

Ebony Nicole

Don't Take….

Don't take shit from me cause you have already taken enough.

You took my virginity but at the end of the day, you didn't take my dignity,

You took my innocence for weakness and I hope you found what you were seeking.

Don't take shit from me cause you have already taken enough….

You took my name and ran it thorough the dirt, trying to put me to shame by

Telling a lie to me face just because you wasn't ready to face the truth but what did I do?

I still tried to protect you from the humiliation I knew you would feel once this secret got out.

Don't take shit from me, you have already taken enough…

Now here we are so many years later and you still can't face the truth, running around

LET GOD FORGIVE HIM

As if your mistakes are going unseen as if what you did to me doesn't mean a thing…

TUH!!...Don't take shit from me, you have already taken enough!!!

Ebony Nicole

~Penetration~

I was eight years eight years old alone, lonely and wanting love from you. You gave me just that since way back as far as I can remember. But, somewhere along the way the love was lost and you were showing me a different light I can remember that morning as if it was yesterday; I was getting ready for school on this hot summer day, you came in the house from a place unknown, you asked me to com up to your bedroom now that, I knew was wrong....

You were my father and I trusted you never thought you would do that horrible thing you did....when we got upstairs you started kissing on me as if I was your woman, like I was old enough to understand...

Then you started to undress me from head to toe and Lord knows I wanted to go, go far away to escape the experience that you were forcing upon me...You laid me on the bed and you penetrated me, you penetrated my virgin walls forcing yourself inside of me. Oh how that brought excruciating pain to my fragile body...

I wanted to scream and beg for somebody...anybody to help me but, what

LET GOD FORGIVE HIM

happened to YOU This used to be your job you crossed that line of no return, you gave up your rights as my father on that morning…do you realize that?..

Do you realize the things that you took from me that I will never get back??...I don't think you do and for this reason we can never start anew…

A new relationship…love or any of that bullshit, you gave all of that away when you

PENETRATED ME!!!

Ebony Nicole

I SURVIVED!!!

I know most people have so many questions to the victims that have been abused; but sometimes there are no answers for those questions. Most times, the only thing that will heal pain is time and when we are not granted enough time, that's when destruction takes place; we began to have all type of different emotions behind what has happened to us. Some days we are happy, some days we are sad…Other days we are mad at the world.

No one will ever understand that, unless they have been abused in some type of way, it is not easy trying to get your life back on track and

LET GOD FORGIVE HIM

do what "Normal People" do…My question is, "What is normal?" I feel normal but what I have encountered sometimes makes me feel indifferent, separated from the rest of the world or is that all in my mind?

Don't get me wrong ***GRATEFUL*** I am because most people don't survive or make it to see another day. God chose me for a reason and I am going to keep pushing forward no matter what. I am strong and wise beyond my years but I'm always humble; I want my experience to help someone else that feel as if they can't make it through another day, read my pain and see how it can change your life.

Somebody is need of something right now and

I just want to be a part of that ***CHANGE!!*** You can make it; you will have your own ***TESTIMONY*** waiting for you at the finish line.

~About the Author~

Ebony Nicole grew up in Atlanta GA but currently reside in Decatur Georgia. Her passion for writing extended from her love for poetry which she has been writing since the age of twelve.

In November 2011 her first book entitled "Let God Forgive Him" (Based on a True Story) was published followed by her second book, "Destiny Is All I Need" in 2012. These were followed by her poetry book "Penetration of a Soulful heart" which was released September, 2013 as well as Ebony Nicole's Encouraging Words.

She has many projects to come and

looking forward to networking and meeting new people along the way.

LET GOD FORGIVE HIM

Ebony Nicole Writes

Destiny Is All I Need:

Destiny thinks she has it all. At one point in her life she was in control. It wasn't until she stepped outside of her relationship that her life took a dramatic turn! Having a good woman by her side wasn't enough, she had to fall into the arms of temptation. Sometimes it's best to keep things simple and sweet but not for Destiny, she wanted more.

Ebony Nicole

Penetration of a Soulful Heart:

My passion for writing extended from poetry. I love to write what my heart feels and through my words I want to inspire others. Inspire them to love, not only themselves but the people around them. Life is full of different emotions and through my poetry you will see some of mine. Every day will not feel like a walk in the park but, it's worth living. These are my sacred feelings but now it's time for the world to get a closer look at who I am. I hope that someone else will find healing and peace in these poems that I share. I want them to make it through one more day. Welcome to Ebony Nicole's World of Poetry.

You Can't Weather My Storm
Prologue:

I was sixteen years old when my mother was killed. I can remember the day like it was yesterday. I was on my way home from school when my cell phone rung. It was my sister, Tracey, telling me I needed to get home as soon as possible. She said there had been a terrible accident. My mind was racing as I quickened my steps; it seemed as if my feet couldn't move fast enough. I wanted to know what had happened to her and who had murdered my mother. In my mind there was nothing that she could have done to cause someone to kill her. She had my sister and me to look after and we loved her. Our lives wouldn't be the same without her and we found that out the hard way. My sister and I had made it through some rough ass times but at the end of the day, she never left my side. She had become my mother, father and everything else I needed. Tracey gave me the game like our mother gave it to her. Everybody in the streets called our mother "Chocolate Desire" but before we knew what she did in the streets, the only name we knew was Cassandra Goode. She was our mother and we were never allowed to talk about what she did, how she did it or who she did it with. She made this very clear and we never went against what she told us. Whenever there was a problem she would handle it and made sure that we didn't hear too much about the bad things that happened. See my mother was a Whore and she made sure everything she did had a price on it. Nothing in this world was free, not even the air we breathe. I can remember her telling me this and I never understood what she meant. By the time I had been around the block a few times, I understand it clearly.

LET GOD FORGIVE HIM

Chapter 1:

Learning the Game Four Years Later

In my sister's book there were two rules to the game: Always get paid and never get pregnant. That was simple because I wasn't trying to be caught up like that; I knew too many that had already fallen victim. They wanted these dudes to love them, take care of them and give them everything their hearts desired. But they were naive as hell if they thought it would end like that. I wasn't asking for all of that, all I needed was the money. I let them know off top what I wanted, that way it would be no misunderstandings.

Tonight would be no different; Tracey and I were getting ready to do what we did best. Tricking off had become the way of life for us and we had no shame in doing it. It paid our bills and we didn't want for shit. As I stood in the mirror looking over my 5'1 frame I had to give myself a pat on the back. I had a body to die for, a round ass, thick thighs and nice set of racks that sat up perfectly for the world to see. "Mia get your ass out of the mirror you are going to make us late." My sister said as she walked into my bedroom. "Shut up, you know I have to make sure I'm on point when we hit the streets. "You know you got that don't even worry about it. You got your looks from mama, no need to worry. Now come on let's roll.

I followed my sister to the front door she was walking fast and I was wondering why she was in so much of rush tonight. Usually we set up our own dates and called all the shots. I started to wonder if these were some new clients that she hadn't told me about. In my mind I was hoping that it wasn't because I was not doing shit extra. These niggas had to be paying more money for all of that.

We made our way to my car and I threw her the keys. Tracey always made fun of my car, saying it was specially designed for short people but, I

LET GOD FORGIVE HIM

didn't care tonight she would be taking the wheel. I made myself comfortable in the passenger seat as she pulled out of the driveway. I allowed my mind to relax a bit as I took in the beautiful sight of downtown Atlanta. It was so beautiful and this was one of the reasons I wanted to live in this area. Sometimes I would sit on my balcony and watch all of the lights that lit up the city at night. But there was nothing like the morning times; watching the sun rise.

My mind was in another place and I could see Tracey glancing my way every now and then. She was the closet person to me and the only one that truly understood me. We made it off the highway, taking the Camp Creek exit. Darrell and Tyrone lived in the area; two of our top paying clients. We had met them a few months ago but they were cool and we really enjoyed the time we spent with them. Besides being sexy as ever they knew how to hold a conversation. They were brothers and it made Tracey and I feel better when we first met.

One of our rules was that we had to be together for most of these dates; that way we could look out for each other at all times. In this line of work, we couldn't afford to take any chances. Everybody couldn't be trusted but one thing I knew for sure, my sister had my back.

*****

Darrell opened the door when he heard us pull up in the drive way. I could see his pearly white smile from a mile away and it turned me on. He stood there shirtless with all of those muscles, just waiting to be touched. His skin was the color of milk chocolate; eyes a deep brown that made me melt with each look he gave me. He always kept his hair cut low but, he had waves for days and I could tell he took pride in his

LET GOD FORGIVE HIM

appearance.

Now his brother Tyrone was the opposite of him when it came to their looks. But he was sexy as a muthafucka too; I was just not the type of woman who liked light skinned guys. That was Tracey's preference and that's why they worked out perfectly. Plus he was a little on the short side which was obvious whenever he and Darrell stood side by side. One quality that I did like about Tyrone was his dreads; they flowed down his back and complimented his hazel eyes.

We entered their home and it was spotless as usual. I loved the setup of their home; they had beautiful art paintings along the walls, a leather sectional in the middle of the floor and a flat screen T.V sat in front of it with a surround sound. When we first visited them, it amazed me at how well they kept their house up. This told me a lot about the two in general. We made ourselves comfortable while they went to the kitchen to fix our drinks. Tonight was going to be a lovely night, I could already feel it...

To be continued in *"You Can't Weather My Storm'* the Novel.

Let God Forgive Him & Destiny Is All I Need can both be ordered from: Amazon, OR directly from me: Writerebonynicole@gmail.com

Penetration of a Soulful Heart can be ordered via Create space, Amazon or directly from me.

Social Media Contact Information:
Facebook:
http://www.facebook.com/profile.php?id=100000039653789
Twitter:
https://twitter.com/#!/EbonyOnTheRise

Author's Fan Page:
http://www.facebook.com/pages/On-The-Rise/174064429351176

www.ingramcontent.com/pod-product-compliance
Lightning Source LLC
Chambersburg PA
CBHW020014050426
42450CB00005B/470